REBUILDING AFTER DIVORCE

NEPHETIA BROWN

CONTENTS

In dedication to my Lord God, Jesus Christ. God, I thank you for allowing me to go through such heartache, to have me meet you where you are!

Thank you for placing such substantial people in my life to help me heal, push me, and pray for me. Prayer came from people that had little to no idea about the change in my life, and I am grateful.

Thank you, God, for my family and loved ones who stood beside me while I was at my lowest point. I was not always easy to deal with, and I understand that. I just truly love them because they did not have to see me through.

I LOVE YOU, LORD, with every ounce of me. I cannot thank you enough!

INTRODUCTION

For those who never thought they'd make it through the night...

In a million years, I never thought that I'd be here sharing a word with you. Yes, you! I am Nephetia Brown, an East New York, Brooklyn girl. I'm loving, a bit rough around the edges, funny, educated, beautiful, and full of JOY...and I'm still standing!

You see, life will shake you and try to break you. But, God sees that His blessings are great and that nothing will ever supersede that. When life happens, we tend to focus on everything wrong, everything that did not happen for us, every negative thing. We forget about all that God has already blessed us with.

In my journey dealing with divorce, I had to remember that God had blessed me with a business, a career, my beautiful sons, and a LIFE! God gave me a life to live, and I had to show Him how much I appreciated it. I remembered to be kind to myself, continue to love, and move toward my destination! I had to live again!

Rebuilding After Divorce is a devotional and journey journal that I am sharing from the heart to relate to those who have gone through and may be going through divorce or separation. It focuses on healing and rebuilding your life, focus, and purpose. I also considered those willing to do extra work before calling it quits. Truly, marriage is a beautiful thing. We just need help, at times, keeping it beautiful. Getting through tough times is best when you can get through with someone who's been in your shoes, and I am delighted to walk with you!

"Gracious words are a honeycomb, sweet to the soul and healing to the bones."

— PROVERBS 16:24 (NIV)

SEASONS CHANGE

Torturous rumbling arose in my body like a thunderstorm
Crashing and clashing against the skies
Winds with nowhere to go but inside
Inside of me like a raging battlefield
And I am unable to move

Unstable on my feet
I take one step and realize I haven't moved at all.
My mind is on the edge
And my heart is jumping from the highest waterfall.
Out of control, my life spins like a tornado
Violently picking up emotions I never thought existed.
I take another step.
Nothing.
And another.
Nothing.
God, please lead me to my rainbow.

CHAPTER 1

IF LOVE COULD

I f love could grab us by the hand and tell us how much it loves us just so that we understand how much we are valued, it would. When an agonizing situation occurs in our lives, such as divorce, we forget how important we are and begin to diminish into agony. The agony will begin to process and become despair. And despair often leads to desperation and, later on, depression. It is very understandable. No one gets married and foresees divorce happening. Transparent moment: I used to believe that prenups were predicting divorce to occur. I know now that it is not.

A prenuptial agreement is a contract you and your spouse enter before getting legally married. They are set to protect both parties' assets in case of divorce or death. I would feel awkward going into marriage thinking there is a possibility of it coming to an end. However, we do have to go into marriage with the love of God. If it doesn't work and our spouse is no longer there, physically, mentally, or spiritually, we know God is there. When we pray to God in despair and agony, trust me, He is there, even if, at that moment, we can't hear or feel Him. Trust that God is replacing the hell in our lives with an everlasting love because that HE IS!

❀

Prayer

Dear Lord, with tears in my eyes and despair in my heart, I ask you to hold me until this hell is over. God, please hold my hand and remind me of what love is, even if I do not want to be reminded. In your precious name, I pray, AMEN.

"Love is patient, love is kind. It does not envy, it does not boast, it is not proud. It does not dishonor others, it is not self-seeking, it is not easily angered, it keeps no record of wrongs. Love does not delight in evil but rejoices with the truth. It always protects, always trusts, always hopes, always perseveres."

— 1 CORINTHIANS 13:4-7 (NIV)

Think about this:

1. What conflicts you from feeling or giving love after things go wrong?

_____

_____

_____

_____

_____

_____

2. How can keeping love in your heart help you heal?

_____

_____

_____

_____

_____

_____

CHAPTER 2
TRUTH IS

The hard truth is that something went wrong along the way, and no one stopped to fix it. You both forgot that you are not just married to one another but that you are in covenant with God. Life gets away from us all. And when there are children to take care of, parents that may have become ill, bills, work, and not enough time spent one on one, you forget to take a step back and reevaluate your relationship. It happens. But what should not happen is forgetting that God is the head of your life and, therefore, at the head of your marriage. The great thing is that God is ALWAYS there to rebuild.

Prayer

Lord, I thank you! I thank you for your forgiveness. I thank you for being my rock. I thank you for not forgetting about me as I did you. Thank you for accepting my apology and giving me the strength to tell you my heart's truth. I thank you for ALWAYS being GOD. AMEN.

"Give thanks in all circumstances; for this is God's will for you in Christ Jesus. Do not quench the Spirit. Do not treat prophecies with contempt but test them all; hold on to what is good, reject every kind of evil. May God himself, the God of peace, sanctify you through and through. May your whole spirit, soul and body be kept blameless at the coming of our Lord Jesus Christ. The one who calls you is faithful, and he will do it."

— 1 THESSALONIANS 5:18-24 (NIV)

Think about this:

1. What in your life do you think you can make adjustments to?

_____

_____

_____

_____

_____

_____

2. How can this help you turn things around in your relationship?

_____

_____

_____

_____

_____

_____

3. How do you think these changes will help turn your life around moving forward?

_____

_____

_____

_____

_____

_____

CHAPTER 3

GOTTA SAVE FACE!

When things were getting really bad in my relationship, I remembered feeling so helpless and unsure of myself. Because I took offense when arguing, hated the cold shoulders, and always felt dismissed, I became extremely insecure and constantly second-guessed myself. But I couldn't let people see what was going on. And I didn't want people feeling sorry or talking badly about my marriage because I was certain we would get it all together.

So when others were around, I'd try to laugh more, entertain, keep him with whatever he asked for, and take care of the kids, all to keep busy because if I didn't, I'd fall apart. This continued for a few months until the lining thinned and things seeped through. To save face, I began to push everyone away. I was severely lonely and almost out of my mind.

But then, one day, I was visiting my mom, and I started talking. And do you know what she said? She knew already! She already saw the change in me and the relationship. All I could do was laugh because it became clear that I was attempting to hide the obvious. Hiding the truth is so unnecessary because the only thing we do is prolong the help that we need. No matter how big or small the situation, you're continuously hurting yourself when you hide the truth from others because, ultimately, you're hiding it from yourself.

⚜

Prayer

God, please stop me from trying to save face. Help me see that I'm hurting more than helping the situation. Guide me to the sources that I need to get the situation rectified. Father, allow me to hear your voice and follow your path so that I can see the light at the very end of what seems like a dark tunnel. I know you are here for me. And you put others in place to be there for me as well. Help me, dear Lord, to see that. In your precious name, I pray, Amen.

"Then you will know the truth, and the truth will set you free."

— JOHN 8:32 (NIV)

Think about this:

1. What truths are you hiding at this present time?

_____

_____

_____

_____

_____

_____

2. How can you rectify your situation instead of hiding it?

_____

_____

_____

_____

_____

_____

CHAPTER 4

WHY ME?

Heartbreak, for some, can be worse than physical pain because it takes forever to go away. With physical pain, whether a broken bone or deep wound, with time, it will heal. That area on your body may be different, but the pain will disappear. But heartbreak is a bit different.

When the heart is broken, the slightest thing can trigger that feeling. A song, a period of time, pictures, all of these things can trigger heartbreak. In fact, when we think we've gotten over a particular area of heartbreak and we are triggered, those triggers can set us back days if we allow it.

But instead of being overwhelmed with pain and asking, "Why me?", let's ask ourselves, "Why not me?" and turn our pain into something great. Easier said than done. I get it. But we can use that time for things we said we didn't have time for. Write the book, travel, catch up with friends, go to that concert, take that cooking class or redecorate your space. Turn that pain into the most PASSIONATE time of your life! Remember that all things work together for the good of those who love God! Be certain to find your passion in the midst of your pain.

֍

Prayer

Dear God, are you listening? I don't want to be in this heartbreak, God. I want to live my life to the fullest, but I do not know where to start. Order my steps so that I may think clearly. Mend my heart so that I can move on. I am so tired of asking, "Why me?" I want to be better, look better and feel better. I want to move on and discover things about me that only you know. I want to live passionately in you, dear God. I want to be the very best that I can be in you. The desire to live passionately is in me because you placed it there. And for that, I thank you. In the name of your son, I pray. AMEN.

"Since Jesus went through everything you're going through and more, learn to think like him. Think of your sufferings as a weaning from that old sinful habit of always expecting to get your own way. Then you'll be able to live out your days free to pursue what God wants instead of being tyrannized by what you want."

— 1 PETER 4:1-2 (MSG)

Think about this:

1. Are you willing to live in sorrow for the rest of your life?

_____

_____

_____

_____

_____

_____

2. Are you willing to be labeled bitter and broken?

_____

_____

_____

_____

_____

_____

3. What steps can you take toward living a full life?

_____

_____

_____

_____

_____

_____

CHAPTER 5
CHANGING FACES

Sometimes, your heart will be in the right place, and all the wrong outcomes will occur. Hurt feelings will cause us to say and do some things that we may look back on later and regret. When you lead with emotion, often, mistakes are made because we do what we feel. Not to say that feelings are wrong, but our emotions may steer us wrong because we all know FEELINGS are temporary. They switch on and off when we are at our angriest, saddest, happiest, etc.

When making decisions that you know may be based upon your emotions, ask God for a sound mind and a clean heart. From there, you will be able to understand your feelings at that moment. When we are going through, we can only see what is before us. The bigger picture gets lost, and we lose focus on what's most important. In enhanced emotion, step back and assess the situation. Ask yourself if what you're about to say or do will represent your best you!

Prayer

Father God, I ask that you help me in my decision-making concerning my children and my household as I seek guidance over my life. I want to lead with a sound mind and heart as I go forward. There are going to be some very tough situations I must face. But I know that only you can steer me in the right direction. In your matchless name, I pray. Amen.

"Trust in the LORD with all thine heart; And lean not unto thine own understanding. In all thy ways acknowledge him, And he shall direct thy paths."

— PROVERBS 3:5-6. (NIV)

Think about this:

1. Why are you emotional?

_____

_____

_____

_____

_____

_____

2. Although your emotions may be validated, what can you do to change how you feel at this moment?

_____

_____

_____

_____

_____

_____

3. Will it benefit or hurt you?

_____

_____

_____

_____

_____

_____

CHAPTER 6

LOUD SILENCE

Sometimes we think we are in a state of being still and letting God take control. But when, "being still" is driven by PURE emotion, all it really translates into is loud silence. We've all heard the saying, "Your silence speaks volumes," right? Usually, when someone says that, they can literally hear what a person is feeling without them speaking about it. Their feelings radiate from them.

When we need to be still in God, HE commands us to wait on His Word by not pushing anything by what we feel and believe should happen. Feelings cause us to react and sometimes overreact. If we focus on the situation at hand, pick it apart, and understand its importance, we will be better at hearing God and being still in Him. The key is not to let anything take you to a place where an action is unforgiven and an apology may be unacceptable.

Prayer

Dear God, I know I am frustrated, angry, and hurt. But I want so bad to hear you speak. I want to be in your presence. I want to feel your calm. God, please show me how to go from a loud silence to a divine stillness in you. Set me free from a cluttered mind. I give you the load and my burden, dear Lord. In your name, I pray, AMEN.

"And he arose, and rebuked the wind, and said unto the sea, Peace, be still. And the wind ceased, and there was a great calm."

— MARK 4:39 (KJV)

Think about this:

1. What was the turning point in your relationship?

_____

_____

_____

_____

_____

_____

2. Was it, or is it being addressed?

_____

_____

_____

_____

_____

_____

3. How can you better communicate how you're feeling?

_____

_____

_____

_____

_____

_____

CHAPTER 7

THE BLIND EYE

I remember ignoring what I saw going wrong. I remember literally justifying actions and comments that were very hurtful to me. And this is not to focus on anyone else's fault. But I am saying that the more we do not address, the more other situations occur and become toxic in a relationship. You feel misunderstood, unappreciated, and resentful when you carry things around without discussing them with your spouse.

During separation and divorce, you're saying, "If only I would have mentioned how they made me feel… If only I would have stopped them in their tracks when they said those things to me. If only…" It's never one person's responsibility to do the work in a marriage. Just like the situation hurt your feelings, your spouse could have been hurting, which led to miscommunication. It's important to be upfront about our feelings so that we are not caught off guard by an untamed tongue.

Prayer

Father, I ask that you allow me not to turn a blind eye to things that may damage me in the future. I ask that You allow me to forgive myself for accepting that behavior, and I ask you to forgive the actions or the behavior that hurt me. Father, I ask that you allow me to express my feelings more often than not. And I ask that you increase my capacity to communicate thoroughly and respectfully in future situations in Jesus' name. AMEN.

"With the tongue we praise our Lord and Father, and with it we curse human beings, who have been made in God's likeness. Out of the same mouth come praise and cursing. My brothers and sisters, this should not be. Can both fresh water and salt water flow from the same spring? My brothers and sisters, can a fig tree bear olives, or a grapevine bear figs? Neither can a salt spring produce fresh water."

— JAMES 3:9-12 (NIV)

Think about this:

1. Are you carrying a burden that is not yours alone?

_____

_____

_____

_____

_____

_____

2. Can someone share the responsibility of carrying that burden with you?

_____

_____

_____

_____

_____

_____

3. How can you diminish the burden?

_____

_____

_____

_____

_____

_____

CHAPTER 8

GET YE BEHIND ME

When we are going through, it's normal to confide in others about our troubles. Our friends and family, out of love, will give you advice that may not be beneficial to you. Hear me, they mean well and want to see you better. But seeing you hurt will cause them to act and speak out of emotion. So take your words to the Lord.

You cannot allow others' opinions and feelings about your situation cause you to stumble. Press forward and look to God for answers. Ask Him to guide you and pray for those in your life that may be hurting for you. Pray that your turmoil won't become theirs. Pray that they will continue to show you love as you press on!

Prayer

Lord, I ask that you guide my heart at this time. Lord, guide my loved ones as they are standing beside me as I go through these trying times. Guide their tongue and emotions so that I can heal as YOU see fit. Let not the enemy seep into our hearts and minds to react or speak foolishly. In your precious name, I pray, AMEN.

"Jesus turned and said to Peter, "Get behind me, Satan! You are a stumbling block to me; you do not have in mind the concerns of God, but merely human concerns."

— MATTHEW 16:23 (NIV)

Think about this:

1. Will what you tell your family or friends benefit your situation?

_____

_____

_____

_____

_____

_____

2. Are you looking for a reaction from them?

_____

_____

_____

_____

_____

_____

CHAPTER 9

FALSE FORGIVENESS

We notice everything that is wrong and nothing that is right, blaming all the things that happened, things said, and things displayed. A feeling of emptiness and being unloved. The feeling of being lied to and hurt. The judgment and excuses. There could be many reasons for divorce, but what about all the reasons to forgive yourself? Forgiving yourself means allowing time to rebuild the life that you deserve.

Do not straddle the fence when it comes to forgiveness! God wants you to give yourself another chance. You are His child, and He has MORE for you. More life to live, more success to maintain, more time to raise your children. MORE! But you have to have faith that MORE is possible.

Prayer

Father God, I thank you for knowing that my life is greater than my circumstances. I thank you for giving me another chance to live every day. Another chance to get it right, another chance to get ME right, Father God. Give me the strength to forgive myself, God. Give me the strength to move on. In your precious name, I pray, AMEN.

"And God shall wipe away all tears from their eyes; and there shall be no more death, neither sorrow, nor crying, neither shall there be any more pain: for the former things are passed away."

— REVELATIONS 21:4 (KJV)

Think about this:

1. If you could forgive yourself for anything related to or unrelated to your relationship, what would it be?

_____

_____

_____

_____

_____

_____

2. Would it put you on the path to rebuilding your life?

_____

_____

_____

_____

_____

_____

CHAPTER 10

IT SHOULD'VE BEEN ME!

I remember how annoyed I was finding out that my ex was moving into a new home with his new wife. I could remember saying, "It should've been me." Not to mention, I was moving into a new home with my entire immediate family! So I was ecstatic and excited, but I still had that little feeling that 'it should've been me!'

And then, as quickly as I thought it, God whispered to me, "NO! It shouldn't be you! I placed you where I needed you to be!" An instant smile appeared across my lips and on my face because I knew that to be true. I was at some of my weakest points in my marriage and had I remained that weak, I wouldn't be here!

We forget that all things happen for a reason. He gives us no more than we can bear. We say these things as if they're cliché. Guess what? They're not. They still stand true! Check this out. If I hadn't gotten a divorce, this devotional would be unavailable to you! Smile! Life is still grand, and He (God) is still using you despite the circumstances. All things work for His good! Remember that!

❦

Prayer

Lord, I only see what is presented to me by others. I don't see what's happening behind their closed doors. But I do know what happens between you and me behind mine. I AM GRATEFUL, GOD! I am stronger and wiser than I've been in the past, and I know I'm right where you need me to be! You get all of the praise, Lord, and I love you for it! In your precious name, I pray, AMEN!

"Let your conversation be without covetousness; and be content with such things that ye have: for he hath said, I will never leave thee nor forsake thee."

— HEBREWS 13:5 (KJV)

Think about this:

1. If it is supposed to be yours, wouldn't it be?

_____

_____

_____

_____

_____

_____

2. Do you feel punished or forgotten about?

_____

_____

_____

_____

_____

_____

3. How can you move on from these feelings?

_____

_____

_____

_____

_____

_____

CHAPTER 11

BUT I'M LONELY

A fter years of being with the one you thought would be your forever, sharing space, intimacy, and love, you find yourself alone. An empty space, a void desperately in need of being filled. It's so difficult to get past that feeling. In reality, we aren't ever alone, but it doesn't feel that way. No one, even those that have gone through divorce and separation, can ever imagine or understand how YOU feel at this very moment. (Or so we think) SMILE!

This feeling is temporary. And we have to truly thank God for that! Because only through him will our hearts heal enough to make us feel at peace with being "alone." Being alone means we have more time to spend with God. Being alone means we have more time to set goals, think them through and execute them. In your alone time, find time to take care of you! Loneliness is temporary. Allow God to step in and refill your spirit.

Prayer

Dear Lord,

I surrender all unto you. I know that my relationship with my spouse has ended, but this void I know can only be filled by you, Father. I understand that this feeling is temporary and that I cannot make decisions based on what is temporary. Guide me, God. Show me the way. Show me what lies ahead so I can make my way through this. Show me how to love and appreciate ME again, God. In your name, I pray, AMEN.

"I have told you all this so that you may have peace in me. Here on earth you will have many trials and sorrows. But take heart, because I have overcome the world."

— JOHN 16:33 (NLT)

Think about this:

1. What makes you feel alone?

_____
_____
_____
_____
_____
_____

2. Have you had negative thoughts about being alone?

_____
_____
_____
_____
_____
_____

3. How can you turn those thoughts around for your good?

_____
_____
_____
_____
_____
_____

CHAPTER 12

WHAT ABOUT THE CHILDREN?

As adults, we are so focused on how we are feeling at the moment about the break in our relationship. We forget to consider how our children may feel and reflect our negativity onto them. We may say things that shouldn't be said about our spouse or act in a way the children should not see.

We say and do things that affect the children and never take the time to think about how the children are feeling. The children are going through this divorce as well. It is just as painful or more painful for them to go through this life-changing event. You want to set a good example for your children by showing them that things will not always be what you want them to be, but getting through the difficult points will build character and reinforce your faith.

Show your children that adults can agree to disagree, therefore doing the right thing to allow your children to move forward peacefully. By making this transition easier on your children, you will witness that you will make it a bit easier on yourself.

Prayer

LORD! Hear my cry! We have been fighting and arguing over things that have no importance. Not one time did we stop and think about our children. Lord, I thank you for my children. They are a gift and deserve to be treated as such. I ask that you forgive me for allowing my needs to overshadow what my children need. They are going through this tumultuous change as well. And I thank you for giving me another day to get it right with them. In your precious name, I pray, AMEN.

"Train up a child in the way he should go: and when he is old, he will not depart from it."

— PROVERBS 22:6 (NIV)

Think about this:

1. Consider the age(s) of each of your child(ren). Is there a difference in behavior for each child since separation/divorce?

_____

_____

_____

_____

_____

_____

2. Is there anything you and your spouse/significant other can do to help your children adjust to their new life? What can you do to help ease their pain?

_____

_____

_____

_____

_____

_____

CHAPTER 13

ANGER...WITHIN REASON

W hen situations attempt to break us, we are overwhelmed with so many emotions. I remember being overwhelmed with emotions and figuring out why my marriage was on a downward spiral. After crying for days, I woke up incredibly angry one morning. That anger stayed there for days making me irrational and difficult to speak to. My children felt it and stayed away. I was almost infuriated.

After wallowing in days of anger, I sat again and cried. I just sat in my room, drowning in my tears and speaking ferociously at my God. And guess what? He said absolutely NOTHING! NOTHING AT ALL! Do you know why? Because I had ignored Him for days when I CLEARLY heard Him tell me to let go of the anger because it would cause a disconnect between myself, my children, and most importantly, Him!

So when I realized I couldn't hear my Father speaking, I panicked. But then I called one of my spiritual moms, and she just began to pray. She prayed, and I cried some more until my head was cleared. I worshipped and prayed and prayed and worshipped until my heart began to open. And as I did that, God was silent. I thought because I had let my emotions overwhelm me, God gave my family and friends little messages for me.

My children were extra loving, my mom was there to help, and my spiritual moms were tarrying while I thought my ear to Him was broken. Can you imagine feeling disconnected from Him? It's heartbreaking. But through it all, we must know He is ALWAYS right beside us. MY GOD! Listen, we are human. We are going to be angry and full of emotion at times. The important thing is not to stay there!

❧

Prayer

Father God, in the name of Jesus, I ask that you heal my heart and pull me out of this downward spiral of anger. FATHER GOD, I ask that you comfort me. That you care for me. That you increase love in my life. Father, I beg of you, please do not let me stay in this pit of hell. Help me to be able to be angry within reason, recycle it and turn this situation into a lifelong learning experience so that I can help others out of their hell. And finally, God, I just want to thank you in advance for the blessings that will come from this. In your mighty name, I pray. AMEN

"The Lord is my shepherd; I shall not want. He maketh me to lie down in green pastures: he leadeth me beside the still waters. He restoreth my soul: he leadeth me in the paths of righteousness for his name's sake. Yea, though I walk through the valley of the shadow of death, I will fear no evil: for thou art with me; thy rod and thy staff they comfort me. Thou preparest a table before me in the presence of mine enemies: thou anointest my head with oil; my cup runneth over. Surely goodness and mercy shall follow me all the days of my life: and I will dwell in the house of the Lord forever."

— PSALMS 23:1-6 (KJV)

Think about this:

1. Why are you angry? Have you ever done anything out of anger? How did you feel afterward? What was the outcome of that action?

_____

_____

_____

_____

_____

_____

2. Moving forward, how can you handle being angry more wisely?

_____

_____

_____

_____

_____

_____

CHAPTER 14

CHOOSE YOU

S peak life over yourself! Speak greatness! Speak abundance! Choose your words wisely when speaking about YOU! We go through life thinking that we are making different mistakes than everyone else when others have made the same or worse. The mistake is not the issue because they can be made to turn around for our good. But if we continue to badger ourselves for the mistake and speak so harshly about ourselves, that's the biggest mistake of them all. Make your mistakes. If you have to apologize for it, apologize with sincerity, forgive yourself, and MOVE ON! This life is not about mistakes. It is about how we choose to USE those mistakes to be better!

Prayer

Father God, help me to CHOOSE ME every time! Help me forgive myself for what I may have done or said and move on! Father God, help me to forgive myself for the choices I've made. Help me live through them so I can receive the life lesson I put in place for me. That lesson will only make me stronger. It will make me a better me. And I thank you each day for the opportunity to live through it all. Thank you, God! In your name, I pray. Amen.

"For I know the plans I have for you," declares the Lord, "plans to prosper you and not to harm you, plans to give you hope and a future. Then you will call on me and come and pray to me, and I will listen to you. You will seek me and find me when you seek me with all your heart."

— JEREMIAH 29:11-13 (NIV)

Think about this:

1. How can you choose to right your wrongs?

_____

_____

_____

_____

_____

_____

2. How can you choose to be better?

_____

_____

_____

_____

_____

_____

CHAPTER 15

FORGIVE YOURSELF!

I remember this particular day when nothing went right. The babies were up late the night before, and I was exhausted at work. I didn't have anyone to call (so I thought) because I would call my ex-husband during my workday in previous years. I felt so ashamed and so low. I was really mistreating myself these days. I was blaming myself for not doing enough, not making enough money, not being sexy or spontaneous enough, not being a good enough mom, just not enough of anything these days.

I was allowing this divorce to destroy me from the inside out. I was deteriorating, and it showed. I didn't see the same beautiful, vibrant Neph I was used to seeing. Then one Saturday, I got out of bed and had some cleaning therapy. With music blasting and the children dancing and laughing, I found my joy.

Then the next day, I got up, took my little ones to church, and found my peace again. Through the tears and the sermon, I forgave myself. "JESUS!" is all that I could shout! YOU ARE OVERDUE FOR FORGIVENESS! God forgave you a long time ago. Why can't you forgive yourself? Do not let grief consume you. It only delays the process.

※

Prayer

I am shouting from the hills that FORGIVENESS IS MINE! I forgive myself. My mistakes are no more than just that. But I will not wallow in my sorrow or grief, dear God! My relationship is over, but my life is not. And I allow myself to move on in forgiveness. I thank you, God, for granting forgiveness in my heart. Thank you for allowing me to see me for the child you placed on this earth. In Jesus' precious name, AMEN.

"Therefore, if anyone is in Christ, the new creation has come: The old has gone and the new is here!"

— 2 CORINTHIANS 5:17 (NIV)

Think about this:

1. Do you believe that God has forgiven you?

_____

_____

_____

_____

_____

_____

2. What steps can you take to completely forgive yourself?

_____

_____

_____

_____

_____

_____

CHAPTER 16

I AM HEALED

Often, we equate healing with ailments and sickness. We take the proper medication, change eating habits and ask God for his healing virtue. But when it comes to our hearts (emotional, not physical wellness), we very rarely take care of the hurt and disappointment that may cause it to break.

Stop right now and take a minute to acknowledge what you have been through. After you stop and acknowledge it, take a minute to recognize the damage done to your heart. Ignoring your pain will not allow you to get through separation and/or divorce. You have to take time with yourself and even sometimes say aloud that you are hurt. Cry, yell, even tell God that you are mad. Do whatever you need to do to get through the pain (as long as it doesn't cause you or anyone else bodily harm). ACKNOWLEDGE that you need time to heal so that you can pick yourself up and enjoy life after marriage.

Prayer

Father, I thank you. Thank you for giving me the time to heal through this very trying process. I ask that you continue guiding me so I won't become bitter or remain angry. Father, let your healing virtue flow! I need you, Father God! In your precious son's name, I pray, AMEN.

"At once, Jesus realized that power had gone out from him. He turned around in the crowd and asked, "Who touched my clothes?" "You see the people crowding against you," his disciples answered, "and yet you can ask, 'Who touched me?' " But Jesus kept looking around to see who had done it. Then the woman, knowing what had happened to her, came and fell at his feet and, trembling with fear, told him the whole truth. He said to her, "Daughter, your faith has healed you. Go in peace and be freed from your suffering."

— MARK 5:30-34 (NIV)

Think about this:

1. What have I done to further my healing process?

_____

_____

_____

_____

_____

_____

2. Have you asked God how to heal?

_____

_____

_____

_____

_____

_____

CHAPTER 17

A FRIENDLY HEALING

W hile talking to God, a dear friend texted me and told me she had just broken up with her love. In complete concern, I called her and was greeted by tears and sobbing. She was hurt and bothered but knew she deserved better. God knew this conversation was coming, so He gave me flashbacks of conversations I had with other girlfriends who were going through a divorce at the same time as I was.

I always had an encouraging word for my girlfriends. However, they were hurt, and I was hurt at the same time. My words weren't always so kind about their spouse or the family. Not that I hated them, but I was hurt for my girls and also very broken myself having to experience the exact same thing. God told me during these flashbacks that He wasn't giving them to me to guilt trip but to understand and see that so much more is required from my experience.

Do not focus on what was done. Focus on what the result must be. Goodness is required in ALL that you do! And this very morning, that was what was required of me when my good girlfriend needed me. As Christians, we must remember that we are to set an example as Jesus did. Kindness and goodness always. Have courage, move forward, and help others when needed. Do not forget to seek God when you're a friend. Jesus' love will flow through you. Pray and focus on the situation at hand.

❧

Prayer

Lord, I thank you for allowing me to be a friend. But please, keep me covered in my friendships so I may lead with a heart like yours. Let me remember that you are first IN ALL THINGS and that your love will shine through me through prayer and supplication. In your everlasting name, I pray. AMEN.

"Two are better than one, because they have a good return for their labor: If either of them falls down, one can help the other up. But pity anyone who falls and has no one to help them up. Also, if two lie down together, they will keep warm. But how can one keep warm alone? Though one may be overpowered, two can defend themselves. A cord of three strands is not quickly broken."

— ECCLESIASTES 4:9-12 (NIV)

Think about this:

1. How can you ask God for help when friends are asking for advice?

_____

_____

_____

_____

_____

_____

2. How can you be a stronger Christian so that when adversity comes along, you can handle it?

_____

_____

_____

_____

_____

_____

CHAPTER 18

AVAILABLE TO YOU

I have a ROUGH time being vulnerable. By definition, vulnerable means to be susceptible to physical or emotional attack or harm. So being vulnerable is no place that I'd like to be.

After my divorce, I vowed not to let people get too close or put me in a position where I could be hurt or taken advantage of. But recently, I realized that by blocking vulnerability, I was disallowing the most important being to enter my heart and mind… MY GOD! I realized that I do not have to allow myself to be taken advantage of, but I have to keep my heart and spirit open to give and receive love.

In doing so, you take the chance of your feelings being hurt. But thank God feelings are temporary. You can work your way through being hurt, but can you work your way through it without God? For me, the answer is and will always be no. Be vulnerable to the spirit, and you will always receive the discernment you need to get through anything.

Prayer

Lord, give me the space to be open and honest about my feelings. And then, Lord, give me space in my spirit to process and deal with those feelings. Please, Lord, keep me open to new possibilities. Keep my mind and heart open to others so I can continue receiving the Holy Spirit. In your precious name, I pray, Amen.

"I am the vine, ye are the branches: He that abideth in me, and I in him, the same bringeth forth much fruit: for without me ye can do nothing...As the Father hath loved me, so have I loved you: continue ye in my love."

— JOHN 15:5-9 (KJV)

Think about this:

1. How can shutting yourself off from vulnerability benefit you? How can it hinder you?

_____

_____

_____

_____

_____

_____

2. Weigh your pros and cons.

_____

_____

_____

_____

_____

_____

CHAPTER 19

REVAMP YOUR LIFE!

When relationships go sour, often, we say and do things to cause an even bigger situation. It's bad enough the marriage is over. Now we have to worry about giving people other things to speculate and talk about by giving them exactly what they are looking for (insert drama, lol). I made this mistake. I was so hurt and broken that I made a few scenes. I wanted to prove how RIGHT I was, to show how hurt I was. Wrong move. The only one I needed to let know the details was my Lord and Savior.

It's good to express how we feel. However, everyone does not have to hear it. Focusing on my health, career, children, and hobbies helped me get through the pain of divorce. The process may be grueling initially, but it's all about getting to where feelings are temporary. God is FOREVER!

Prayer

God, please do not allow these temporary feelings to consume me. God, I promise to work hard not to allow how I feel to get in the way of what you have for my Life. I am hurting, Lord! However, I have to let go and allow you to work it out. I thank you in advance for my healing Lord. In your son's precious name, AMEN.

"That means you must not give sin a vote in the way you conduct your lives. Don't give it the time of day. Don't even run little errands that are connected with that old way of life. Throw yourselves wholeheartedly and full-time—remember, you've been raised from the dead!—into God's way of doing things. Sin can't tell you how to live. After all, you're not living under that old tyranny any longer. You're living in the freedom of God."

— ROMANS 6:12-14 (MSG)

Think about this:

1. Think about the things you loved to do before you were married. Which things did you place on the back burner that you would love to pick up and continue with?

_____

_____

_____

_____

_____

_____

CHAPTER 20

LET YOUR LIGHT SO SHINE

The loneliness, the anger, the pain, and the disappointment can take you to places so far away from who you are that you would have never imagined, in a million years, that this would be your life. It is not to say that these feelings aren't warranted. However, you should not reserve a seat to remain there. You can never manifest the visions God has given to you if you decide to engulf yourself in a downward spiral of would've, could've, should've. And yes, we all know that marriage is honored by God. But God knows us best, and He forgives our mishaps and mistakes.

We have to take our issues to him and live our lives to our fullest potential. God grants us forgiveness. Therefore we should also grant forgiveness to those that may have hurt us. We have to remember that forgiveness is for us! Without it, we will never be able to heal and move forward. So, I encourage you to MOVE FORWARD! Get your healing on, and LET YOUR LIGHT SHINE! Remind folks that God has sustained you and has ordained you to live a life of ABUNDANCE! Now get to it! Your new life awaits!

※

Prayer

Lord! I thank you for opening my heart and mind to newness. I thank you for opening my heart and mind to forgiveness. I want my life to reflect you and be who you have called me to be. I am excited to live a life full of abundance and joy! I understand there will be good and bad days, but I no longer accept that the bad will outweigh the good. I am ready to move on, and I thank you for it! In your precious name, I pray, AMEN!

"You are the light of the world. A town built on a hill cannot be hidden. Neither do people light a lamp and put it under a bowl. Instead, they put it on its stand, and it gives light to everyone in the house. In the same way, let your light shine before others, that they may see your good deeds and glorify your Father in heaven."

— MATTHEW 5:14-16 (NIV)

Think about this:

1. What visions did God give you for newness?

_____

_____

_____

_____

_____

_____

2. How can you execute these visions?

_____

_____

_____

_____

_____

_____

3. How can you create a new start?

_____

_____

_____

_____

_____

_____

WHEN SILENCE SPEAKS
LOUDER

Heart-wrenching
Gut-wrenching truth
The feeling that no one cares about you.
Tears flow with unaccompanied words
Silence when you know you're speaking words
The feeling of often being unheard.

Sacred vows once set apart
Secrets deep between two hearts
Hidden gems of sacrifice and trust
Unhonored vows now crushed to dust
Silence when you know you're searching for words
The thoughts when you know you're being unheard

A man who gives love you've always waited for
A woman vibrant, full of love you solely adore
A love combined, shared, then scattered at sea
A union no longer handled tenderly.

Waves of silence no longer ignored,
Waves of silence unheard against the shore.

❧

ABOUT THE AUTHOR

❧

Nephetia Brown is a mother of three sons, an electrician, and an author. Once a young single mother and now a divorced single mom, she never saw giving up as an option. As a firm believer in the Holy Trinity, she knew God had something in store for her. Unafraid of affliction, she stands strong in her faith, encouraging women to rebuild their lives after divorce.

The sole purpose of her life is to praise the Lord and be an example in the Lord, according to Psalms 150:6, which states,

"Let everything that hath breath praise the Lord. Praise ye the Lord," and Matthew 5:16, which states "Let your light so shine before men, that they may see your good works, and glorify your Father which is in Heaven."

Nephetia appreciates being used to help her brothers and sisters in Christ. If her testimony can help heal hearts and minds, she will continue to share it until the Lord decides her work on earth is finished.

www.ingramcontent.com/pod-product-compliance
Lightning Source LLC
LaVergne TN
LVHW051811080426
835513LV00017B/1910

The Gay Travel Guide

For

Tops and Bottoms
USA EDITION

By DREW BLANCS

ICON EMPIRE PRESS
Toronto Vancouver New York London
ISBN: 978-1-927124-08-6
All Rights Reserved © 2012
by DREW BLANCS

Published by Icon Empire Press 552 Church Street Toronto, ON
M4Y 2E3 CANADA.

NOTICE

This book is a collaboration of materials compiled by the editor(s). Although all suggestions were given in anonymity, we would like to state with gratitude that all source material is acknowledged. The editor(s) have made their best efforts to ensure that any copywritten material has not been infringed upon in the publishing of this book. All characters are fictitious and any similarities to any real persons or events are simply coincidental and unintended. The views expressed in this book are the views of the authors and do not necessarily reflect the views or policies of the publisher.

ACKNOWLEDGEMENT

I would like to thank Holly Whu, P. Jones, B. Nijjar, T. Tewsley, Dennis Ziebell and Bill Pung, who all helped in the creation of this book.

"Icon Empire Press would like to thank George Smith and Smith Proofreading (www.smithproofreading.com) for their fantastic proofreading and editing services."